Religion in Business and Business in Religion

RELIGION IN BUSINESS

AND

BUSINESS IN RELIGION

Religion in Business

AND

Business in Religion

_BY_

HENRY A. STIMSON, D. D.
PASTOR PILGRIM CONGREGATIONAL CHURCH

ST LOUIS
ALDEN PRINTING CO., PUBLISHERS
1892

Say ye to the righteous that it shall be well with him, for they shall eat the fruit of their doings. Woe unto the wicked. It shall be ill with him; for the reward of his hands shall be given him. Isaiah III. : 10-11.

RELIGION IN BUSINESS.

LET me disclaim at the outset the thought of possess-
ing any special wisdom with reference to business
affairs. I have no prescription for insuring success. Religion in Business does not mean success in business. No
amount of religion will make after-thought serve for fore-
-thought, or erroneous judgment take the place of correct
judgment, or heedlessness do the work of pains-taking,
or ignorance answer for experience. Religion does not
make the small, great; or the simple, shrewd; or the weak,
strong; or the sick, well; or the foolish, wise; at least in
business.

But for all that, God's word abundantly declares that
there is a very close connection between business and
religion. If there is one thing plainer than another in the
Bible, it is that God makes a difference between honesty
and dishonesty, and that He rewards men according to their
deeds. Whatever may be the relative standing of men on
earth, God tries them by their integrity, or want of integrity; and blesses the one while He curses the other.

Here, then, is the ground on which I venture to have
something to say to you. I have not to teach you how to
make money, but how to serve God.

Furthermore, let me say that I know something of your
burdens and perplexities. Far be it from me to make light
of them. Because the world at large knows what are the

temptations of business men, the world gives such high honor to honorable men of business. Christian men are the back-bone of the business community. I well remember when, as a boy, I was a clerk in a great house in New York, hearing a fellow clerk, an infidel and a foreigner, cursing, because in New York, if a merchant was known to be a church member he had better credit. What was it but his unwilling testimony to the fact that the average Christian business man is more trustworthy than the average business man not a Christian? We may praise God that it is so generally true. At the same time we must not be blind to the struggle. All do not stand. Temptations are hot. The pressure is often terrific. Many get involved in doubts and perplexities and weak compromises—many fall. What can we do to clear the vision, to brace the courage, to strengthen the purpose? How can we help one another to serve God bravely each in his place?

Let me put what I have to say in the form of a few propositions, which will, I trust, need little discussion, and may serve to make some things clearer.

First: You will all admit that RELIGION IN BUSINESS IS THE SAME AS RELIGION OUT OF BUSINESS.

When God says, "The soul that sinneth it shall die," He does not add, "except the sin be a commercial sin." When He says, "Thou shalt love the Lord thy God with all thy heart, and thy neighbor as thyself," He does not say "except you are in business." When a man approaching the question of personal religion, feels, as most do, that he must begin to do business differently, his feeling is perfectly correct. There are not two kinds of moral law, one for private life and Sundays, the other for business and week days: one for the pulpit, the other for the street.

Christianity has but one code of morals. I know it is often claimed that there are two, and if this proposition were opened to discussion a good deal would be urged about the necessity of doing business in a different way from that enjoined in the New Testament, and that many Christian men do business in that way. But, when all is said, there remains in your heart the deep conviction that there can be but one right way, and you despise the man who, profess-ing to be a Christian, departs from it. Religion in business is the same as religion out of business.

Second: IF A MAN'S RELIGION DOES NOT KEEP HIM HONEST IT IS WORTHLESS.

This does not mean: " If a man's religion does not keep him as honest as other men are in the same business." Nor: "If a man's religion does not keep him honest where dishonesty is likely to be found out."   It carries the ques-tion back to the forum of a man's own conscience, and the law of God. If a man's religion does not hold him to doing that and that only which is right in God's sight, and which needs no justifying, his religion is so far worth-less. He may be a decent man; he may be a successful man ; he may be an honest man, as the world counts hon-esty, but a religious man, a Christian man—No !

The sole function of religion is to bring a man in heart and life into accord with God, and to keep him there; and any man whose religion does not hold him to that stand-ard, in business or out of it, is self-deceived.

I do not say he may not at last be forgiven. God's un-covenanted mercies are great; but such religion as a pres-ent reality, and as a witness to God, is vain.

Third: THERE IS NO HONEST OCCUPATION IN WHICH AN HONEST MAN IS REQUIRED TO BE DISHONEST.

I speak of honest men, not of those who would like to be honest, but are not.   There are such,—men who approve honesty, who deeply regret that they are in circumstances which compromise them, who mean some day to do differ-ently, and who are very anxious to be taken, like a patent medicine, at their own estimate of themselves. such men, I know, are often engaged in honest occupations in which they think they are required to be dishonest. But I am speaking of honest men; and of them I say that in no honest occupation are they required to be dishonest.

Why! dear friends, God made the world, and He made it right. We are here to till the earth and subdue it. God has established the conditions of successful existence. You talk of the laws of trade. So far as there are laws, i. e., fixed relations from which sound principles of procedure can be deduced, they are as truly God's laws as are the Ten Commandments. God has not made the earth and then left it to be set to any purpose and used for any iniquitous device that man may concoct. It is His world. He is everywhere in it, guiding, controlling, accomplishing with it His own purposes, as truly now as at the beginning.

Despite the loss and confusion from man's wrong-doing, the world is steadily advancing in the accumulations of industry, and all that constitutes temporal progress. Compare our circumstances with those of our ancestors, say five hundred years ago. Their floors had no carpets, their rooms no chairs, their windows no glass, their tables no forks, their houses no books. Society meant the unrestrained dominion of the strong over the weak. The laborer lived in a hovel, slept on the ground, was unshod, and almost wholly unclad. Within the memory of men now living steam, in all its thousand applications, electricity, illuminating gas, coal-oil, stoves, anthracite coal, cheap postage and transportation, dress goods printed from rollers, cheap cotton fabrics, and scores of articles now in common use, have been either invented or given to the world. The average comfort and the average possessions of men have vastly increased, and that despite all that men, by war and crime have done to prevent it. The poorest laborer enjoys many things daily which, one hundred years ago, the wealthiest man could not obtain. Can you suppose for a moment that this vast advance, this steady and rapid accumulation of the best products of industry and skill, is the result of fraud or dishonesty, or is the outcome of obedience to laws, whether they be of trade or of the state, which are antagonistic to the laws of God? Doubtless there is much rascality in the world. Doubtless "because," as of old, "sentence against an evil work is not executed speedily, the heart of the sons of men is wholly set in them to do evil." But two things cannot be denied: that God made the world and men to live in it; and that the world, according to God's plan, is steadily advancing in the accumulations of man's industry and the facilities of man's life. Therefore, progress cannot rest upon dishonesty. The occupations of men by which the world is helped forward, are honest occupations, and honest men can engage in them, and deal honestly.

It is idle for a man to say that he cannot succeed in business and be honest. It is untrue. The whole history of the race is against it. Why have vice and immorality eaten out the heart, and so destroyed nations which the most vigorous foes could not overthrow? It is because vice and immorality arrayed God against them, and the very forces of life and of society, which God has established, and they disregarded or defied, mustered to destroy them.

Is not this just as true of dishonesty as of vice? Where is a single business house that has been built up and stood through the centuries buttressed in dishonesty? There is not one. The very thought is absurd. The hosts of God are arrayed against such business, and sooner or later they hurl it to the ground. Has not the world long since recognized this? Has it not framed for its own selfish ends the maxim "Honesty is the best policy." Victor Hugo said Napoleon failed at Waterloo, not because of the rain the previous night, not because of Grouchy's delay, but because he "*Embarrassed God.*" So business men fail when they think they can insure success by business methods that embarrass God.

Fourth: ANY OCCUPATION IN WHICH A MAN CANNOT BE HONEST, OR THINKS HE CANNOT BE HONEST, AND

SUCCEED, IS FOR HIM A NEFARIOUS OCCUPATION,
AND HE SHOULD QUIT IT.

God does not require that we succeed in what we under-
take. He does require that we maintain our character. If
we find ourselves placed where we cannot do that, our
course is perfectly plain. The occupation, be it what it
may, is for us nefarious. It is of no consequence who may
be in it, or what others may think of the propriety of it; if
you are persuaded that you cannot succeed in the business
in which you are engaged without doing what in your heart
you feel to be dishonest, your duty is, at any cost, promptly
to leave it.

Now, with these propositions before us, which I believe
to be, and which I think you will accept as foundation
truths, let me try to say some things which will strengthen
you against temptation. I believe that LOOSE BUSINESS
HABITS HAVE MUCH TO DO WITH LOOSE BUSINESS
MORALS. What are the loose business habits? They are
numerous. Trusting to luck is one of them ; hoping that
things will come out right when you don't take the trouble
to see that they do ; ignorance as to exact facts ; half un-
derstood and indefinite agreements; carelessness as to
your spoken word; promising to do, or agreeing to do,
what you have no thought of doing exactly ; easy excuses
with yourself for disregarding other people's interests, or
wasting their time in not keeping your appointments to
the minute; that slovenliness in dealing with employes,
which takes no note of idleness and incompetency, and
equally, fails to appreciate fidelity, and to reward valuable
service; overlooking the human element that enters into
all work and trade, and makes a friend worth more than
temporary profit; foolish competition, that thinks it does
not matter how you get your business provided you get it;
untruthful advertising. Do you think a man can exagger-
ate, or tell lies in the newspaper, or in his circulars to his
trade, without becoming careless of truth, and even blind

to truth in other relations? Do you think a merchant can
deceive his customers without teaching his clerks to deceive
both them and him? A self-respecting man does not easily
fall before temptation. A business man, who has himself
well in hand can generally keep his business in hand.

A second snare to business men is MORAL COWARDICE.

Bear with me. I must call things by their right names.
I want to help you if I can. I know something of the
pressure that you are under. You have a family to sup-
port, or a position to establish. You know that for a man
of character to fail is to inflict a more or less serious evil
upon the community It brings Christian character into
question; it does harm to religion. The causes of his
failure may have been entirely beyond his control. The
world only knows that he has made engagements he cannot meet, and his name is dishonored. You are under
obligation, therefore, to succeed.

Moreover, you are in competition with unscrupulous men;
or perhaps you happen to be in partnership with them.
They are found in all departments of business—men who
know no law but self-interest; they care nothing for God;
they have no conscience; they misrepresent goods; they
deceive the public; they hesitate at no mean advantage;
they jump at the chance to do you harm. I know all this.
But for this very reason the temptation to moral cowardice
is strong. The pressure is so great that you are carried away
in spite of yourself. Satan springs upon you sudden temptation. He touches you in the sensitive spot. Your trade
will be injured. A customer may be won away; and in
the fear of thus giving advantage to competitors in a struggle that is so hot you betray yourself. You let down, or
hide your principles. You give place to the devil. It is
perhaps little to be wondered at, but it is none the less
disastrous. A rival manufacturer is adulterating his
goods; how can you afford to sell a genuine article? A
dangerous competitor has opened a line of trade from which

you have scrupulously held aloof. You could strain a point and call it legitimate, but hitherto you have not done it. Your conscience would not let you. But it is very profitable. Or, you can hurry your work up or gain a little advantage by having your clerks work on Sunday, or by getting your mail on Sunday; or you consent to work on Sunday yourself; or you learn that your neighbor has discovered a trick by which he gets great advantage, we will say of the railroad company; his shipping tickets give wrong weights; he overloads cars; he ships goods under false descriptions; he secures wrong classification; he works through a freight clerk and pays commission on surreptitious rebates; or perhaps he has goods to sell, and he bribes the purchasing agent. Now, shall you not do the same? Or, you have suffered loss through fraud or theft, and it will cost you some trouble, and possible further loss to punish the wrong-doer, and do your part toward protecting the community. Or, the community is seeking to rid itself of some public evil, and there is occasion for united protest, and you may lose trade or offend some customer if your name is seen with others, or if your voice is heard on the side of the public welfare. I have known wealthy business men, Christian men, hasten to take their names off such protests, or asseverate that they signed them through a misunderstanding, when they had been published, because they were suddenly ashamed. "We sell our merchandise, not our principles," said one indignant merchant to some customers that waited upon him after such a protest had appeared. The snares of Satan are innumerable, and many a weak and timid soul is beguiled. How cheaply many men sell themselves! But Satan is a coward. I received the other day a communication from a detective agency, which had as a standing heading these words, "Responsible Shadows and Private Watchmen Furnished." That is exactly what is wanted. A responsible shadow! and a private watchman! Christian men who watch the workings of their own thoughts with such a sense of exact accountability that the very beginnings of temptation are discovered, and whose shadow even is responsible. They do nothing, however unwittingly, of which they have reason to be ashamed.

Once more: THE COMMUNITY AT LARGE OWES IT TO BUSINESS MEN THAT THE TEMPTATION TO DIS-HONESTY BE MADE AS SLIGHT AS POSSIBLE.

This in several ways. You should refuse to trade with dishonest men. It is not enough that you are honest yourself. You have not done your whole duty until you strive to make honesty successful by boycotting dishonesty. If a man can cheat you, and still have your custom; if a man can be notoriously untruthful and dishonest, and still hold a large business and make plenty of money, and nobody seem to care so long as they can get goods of him cheap, what wonder that the defense of honest tradesmen is broken down, and business turns into a head-long scramble for shekels.

For the same reason the community owes it to business men that they make the laws such as to remove, and not to increase, the temptation to dishonesty. I have nothing to say as to the inherent desirability and wisdom of the Inter-state Commerce law, but look at the situation to-day. I recently sat in a company of most respectable St. Louis merchants, and heard one of their number say, "You know that three-fourths of you gentlemen could be sent to the penitentiary for what you are doing under that law," and what was the reply? A gentle and genial smile around the circle—not a word, not a look, not a hint of indignant protest at such an amazing charge! A prominent railway official, a gentleman and a Christian, said to me the other day: "It is simply impossible to do business honorably. I have thrown honor to the winds." Think of a community getting into a condition in which its greatest corpora-tions, the railways, and its merchants alike, unite to do business by evasions, and subterfuges, and go-betweens, and secret rebates, and greenbacks carried around in satchels and passed through clerks into the hands of reputable merchants ! Such a system would have made apples and a serpent superfluous in the garden of Eden. It would breed a race of knaves anywhere.

Then, when you have proper laws, you need to set honest men to administer them. Look at the state of things to-day in St. Louis. See the way in which municipal legislation is bought and sold, and reputable business men join in it, because it promotes their schemes. Did ever city endure deeper disgrace than that New Year's Southern Hotel banquet? The representatives of great private corporations dining and wining public officials and bosses, in open, shameless, defiant jubilation over successful corruption and knavery, and with a lively sense of favors to come. "Necessity makes strange bed-fellows." Yes, but think of the plea of such necessity, in this day of grace, in a city of freemen, and on the lips of you merchants, you business men of St. Louis.

Much more might be said. But surely this is enough to show, both how great are the responsibilities of a Christian business man, and how great are his privileges. He is a man chosen of the Lord, and set by Him in the midst of a sinful and rebellious world to witness for Him. Honor and truth and righteousness are on his side. He is in the forefront of the battle. Yes, you dear friends are standard bearers for Christ. What if the conflict is hot? What if the smoke of battle fills the air? What if many fall? "Blessed is the man that walketh not in the counsel of the ungodly, nor standeth in the way of sinners, nor sitteth in the seat of the scornful." "Set yourselves, stand ye still and see the salvation of the Lord with you," is the Lord's voice to you to-day, as it was to the men of old. Only be true to your calling. Remember that there is woe to him that gains an evil gain, for he sins against his own

soul. Watch well your conscience. Respect its question-
ings. Guard yourself against haste to be rich. A large
business is a large trust ; be sure you can be trusted before
you set your heart on the large business. Many a man
loses his head in a high place who walked safely when he
was in a low one. I have known more than one to reverse
the parable. He got along very well so long as the Lord
gave him only one pound; when he found himself possessed
of ten he went to pieces. You wives have a great deal
to do with this. When the wife gets into her head the idea
that her husband is going to be a rich man, and begins to
egg him on, then there is peril. How often your plain,
hard-working, unambitious husband, who was but now
generous, friendly, helpful to all, is seen becoming with
prosperity, close, selfish and vain-glorious. The Lord gives
such people the desire of their heart, and sends "leanness
into their soul." A "snare and many foolish and hurtful
lusts that drown men in destruction and perdition !" It is
well not to be too eager for success. You may be sure of
wealth of character without fear, but wealth and character
come not so surely together. A Christian business man may
well be proud of such success as God gives him ; and may
rightly pray that God will suffer him to die in the harness.
He needs no larger field to fight his fight, and win his
crown for God.

Thou shalt love the Lord thy God with all thine heart, and with all thy soul and with all thy might. Deut. VI.: 5.

What shall it profit a man if he shall gain the whole world and lose his own soul? Mark VIII. : 36.

BUSINESS IN RELIGION.

IF ever there was a time when a line could be drawn
round certain occupations, and it could be said, "Within
this line the rules and methods of business prevail, outside of it they do not," that day has passed. In the
management of the home, the school, the church, there
must be system, order, purpose, in short, a recognition
of business and business ways, or success cannot be ex-
pected.

This being true in the outer and practical life, it has
occurred to me that through its lessons we may get at the
truths of the inner and spiritual life. If business means
so much and accomplishes so much in the world, may it
not have value if we can apply it to religion?

There are certain great principles that underlie all business, and determine success or failure. I have, from time
to time, talked on the subject with many successful business
men, and I am surprised to learn what a striking uniformity
there is in their testimony. Quite independently of what
may be their personal character, or their religious conviction, or their want of conviction, in the main they all agree
as to the principles of business which they regard as essential to success. I am encouraged to believe, therefore, that
these may be helpful in throwing light upon religion.

They all agree in the first place, that to be successful, one
must have a METHOD, a plan, for the conduct of his busi-

ness. To trust to luck, to go at hap-hazard, is sure to end in
failure. Sometimes the plan is adopted instinctively, as
a result of a man's character or his previous training.
One gentleman told me that when they organized their
firm, he and his partners sat down and talked it over carefully, and thus determined the plan by which their business
was to be conducted. But plan there must be. Moreover,
the plan once carefully settled, must be held to. It must
not be changed under stress of weather or adverse circumstances. A leading miller said to me: "Our plan is to
succeed by making the best flour that can be produced.
We believe it is the surest way of success. If things go
against us and some one makes better flour than we do,
we do not rest until we learn how to improve our grade."
Another manufacturer said: "One of our rules is to make
a profit on every order we take. If we find we are losing
orders we don't change our rule, but we study economy
until we discover some way of doing the work at a smaller
cost."

Another one has quite a different rule. He feels the need
of a very wide and large market, and to secure it will often
sell for a time below cost. But whatever the plan adopted,
all agree that to have no plan, or to change one's plan from
day to day, is as disastrous as to change one's business,
and for the same reasons. A man cannot be a grocer this
year, a dry-goods dealer the next, a miller the third, and
hope to succeed. He must commit himself to some one
business, fix his plan for conducting it, and then stick to
it.

Furthermore, I find, in the second place, that all agree
that a man cannot succeed without giving HIS UNDIVIDED
ATTENTION to his business. He must make a business
of it. Very few men can successfully conduct several kinds
of business at the same time. St. Louis is full of men who
have failed from dabbling in things foreign to their legitimate affairs. Outside things can be taken up for

recreation or rest. If they compete with a man's regular business in their demand upon either his thought or his time, they are sure to work him evil. One thing, with all the mind, the heart, the strength, appears to be the rule.

But this requires, in the third place, that a man HAVE A BUSINESS to which he can give himself. He must regard it as worthy of his efforts. He must believe in it, and take pride in it. "We stake all we have on our business," said one man to me. "We draw out of it only enough to live on, and we are living economically. We put all we can into our plant." Others stake everything on their plan of accumulation. They sacrifice comfort, ease, sometimes even friends or character itself, for the chosen line of success. A man can hardly hope to succeed in anything unless he puts his heart into it. He cannot put his heart into it unless he believes in it. A man, therefore, must have some business in which he can believe, and of which, as a measure of his success, he can be proud.

Again, I find, in the fourth place, that SPECIAL TRAIN-ING is regarded as very essential to success in business.

"It is absolutely indispensable in our business," said one merchant. "We have daily to make decisions on the instant, which largely involve our success or failure. No man can do it who is not trained to the business." "Competition," said another, "is now so close that education in business is going to be a more and more important element of success. It did not require much business training when a grocer could make a dollar profit on a sack of flour. It is a different matter when he has to sell it on a margin of a few cents." Many fail from too great haste to get rich. They are not content with slow accumulations; nor are they willing to begin at the bottom and work up. Patient, steady, instructive growth is more important to day than it ever was.

Once more : All agree that to succeed, a man must be prompt to ADAPT HIMSELF TO CHANGES which from time to time take place, both in markets and methods of business.

One manufacturer said to me : "So great are the changes in our business, that I would rather take into my mill a green hand, than one who learned the trade ten years ago and has learned nothing since." Men are everywhere on the look-out for novelties, in fabric, in style, in adapta- tion. A wholesale merchant said : "We used to depend for our trade largely upon advertising. We would soon run out if we did that now. We hunt up customers, and keep after them." Even the banks, they tell me, have greatly changed their methods in recent years.

Again : and this point is somewhat remarkable, in view of what is constantly said about the dishonesty of business men ; I find that our successful business men are doing business on the basis of TRUST IN OTHERS.

One says : "In our business we get security when we can, but a man cannot do business who does not trust somebody." There is no such thing as trusting no one and succeeding, or doing business on an absolute certainty. Another says : "We do business on the basis of our belief that men are honest. We trust those with whom we deal absolutely. Our business rests almost entirely on verbal contracts." Another, of whom I inquired, said : "Cer- tainly ; the basis of our business is the confidence we have in others. We never could have succeeded unless others had had this confidence in us." "This is the whole foun- dation of my business career," said one gentleman, with evident feeling. "If men had not trusted me, I could have done nothing." The tendency of business seems to estab- lish the principle that a man's word is his capital. It is conclusive proof that the entire structure of commercial enterprise is erected on the doctrine of probabilities. Cer- tainty is not required and is not to be had. Faith in one

another, faith in one's judgment, faith in one's principles
and methods of business is the foundation of every successful career. Unless a man is willing to accept this, and
to order his business affairs by a reasonable faith, he cannot do business.

Still further: I find all to agree that ATTENTION TO
DETAILS is a first principle of success. One man said to
me: "We know what every man in our employ is doing,
all the time." Another said: "My partner, or myself, is
familiar with every department of our business. We watch
every man and every process. We keep exact account of
every item." "We attend more closely to detail," said
another, "than any other mill in the country." "I mark
the price on every article in my store," said another. "We
know exactly what every one of our salesmen is making
for us," said still another. A man content with generali-
ties, or who drifts with the crowd, cannot succeed now-a-
days.

Finally: I observe that successful business men ARE
LIBERAL IN THEIR DEALING WITH OTHERS AND EXACT
IN THEIR DEALING WITH THEMSELVES.

One man, who holds himself to the most careful rules,
and prides himself upon his exact accountability, and that
of every man in his employ, says that as a matter of policy,
his firm makes it a rule to settle every claim liberally, even
when it involves temporary loss. It promotes good will
and helps business. Another says: "We give a customer
the benefit of the doubt." And another—though I fear his
kind is rare—"We could get our labor considerably cheaper,
but we want the good-will of our men." It seems to be a
rule of successful business, especially that on the largest
scale, that while a man can hardly be too generous in his
business dealings with others, and that narrowness or
closeness in this relation is sure to defeat itself, in dealing
with oneself a man can hardly be too exacting. He must
know his own purposes: he must constantly revise his

knowledge and keep his experience brought down to date;
he must deny himself in leisure, in lux.ry, in ease; he must
have an aim and plan, and hold to them; he must concen-
trate his mind, his strength, his heart, upon what he has
to do; or he cannot succeed. It is no wonder that when a
man does business in this way he takes pride in his business. He may, at times, get discouraged and talk differ-
ently, but where is there a successful business man, who,
beyond the money he is making, does not take pride in
his factory, his store, his system, his establishment, as
representing himself in his effort to do his best?

There, I believe you have what you will recognize as the
more important principles that underlie successful business
life. The list might easily be enlarged. Doubtless there
are other rules or principles of more immediate application
to your own special affairs. But these are enough, and
they are genuine. Now let me ask you to turn with them
to the matter of religion. You shall judge youselves.

First, answer me this: "What shall it profit a man if he
gain the whole world, and lose his own soul?" Don't
turn away from it. You have said that a man must choose
an object in life and set his heart upon it. You have said
it must be an object worthy of him, worthy of his best
efforts, worthy of all there is in him, or he cannot do his
best, he cannot fairly hope to succeed. Before we go any
further, answer me this, you successful business man,
you young man who would be successful; you have made
your choice, you are in full career, you have staked everything willingly, gladly, on your business or your profession;
tell me, what will it profit you, where will you be at the
end, if you gain all you seek, and lose your own soul?

Again: you have said, a man must have a fixed and
earnest purpose, a plan, clear and intelligent, if he would
succeed in business. How many of you are applying this
principle to religion? I ask you unconverted men, and you
who are contented with a merely nominal religion. Have

you a plan, a purpose? You have wishes—hopes. You mean some day to be a different man from what you are. How different this from your method in the affairs of the world. Where is your honest, manly purpose? Where is the settled plan by which you are approaching steadily, surely, with determination to succeed, the salvation of your soul? You meant once to be a Christian. You once were in earnest. And you have grown cold. You were offended by the conduct of some church member. You did not like what was said in the pulpit. You were not pleased at the prayer meeting. And you are the man who says that a man cannot succeed in business who does not stick to his purpose and hold his plans, no matter what arises to thwart him. You were once in full view of Christ. Where are you now? What is your purpose now?

A man must give his undivided attention to his business if he would succeed in it. Undivided attention! "Ye shall seek for me and find me when ye shall search for me with all your heart." That looks as if the method of religion was very much like the method of business, does it not?

You know the conditions of success in business, and you are only too eager to meet them. Do you meet them, are you meeting them in religion? Why do you go on from year to year in this half-hearted slow-footed way, hanging on the skirts of the sanctuary keeping within reach of the gospel, but without paying any real attention to it—doing nothing to make it real to yourself?

You say, a man, to succeed, must stake something on his business; he must believe in it. How much have you staked on Christ? "If Christ be not risen from the dead, then is our preaching vain and your faith is also vain." Can you say that? Has Jesus Christ risen for you? Have you staked the forgiveness of your sins, and your hope of heaven on Him as a living, present Savior, dwelling in your heart, inspiring and governing your life? Don't put the question aside. Answer it fairly.

You say a man must have training in business. How much have you in religion? Do you really believe your maxim? Is a man's place, is his joy, his usefulness, his growth in spiritual things to be determined, as in business, by his training for these things? Is it true that the nobler the work a man would do, the higher the prize he would win, the more necessary the special training? Is it true that in religion early years are best years, and that a man can never make up for early years thrown away, or bible neglected, or opportunities squandered, or commands of God disobeyed, or God kept far off? Is all this true? Deep in your heart do you know it to be true? and yet you are content to put off becoming a Christian, or content not to be a truer one?

You say a man must be watchful of changes of methods of business. And how many of you are waiting for some old-time experience to come round again! Once you were stirred by some great preacher, and you are patiently waiting now to be stirred by some powerful appeal. Once you were caught up in a great revival and swept on to the very gates of the kingdom. You sit helpless to-day awaiting a return of the wave. Once you were under deep conviction of sin. God strove with you manifestly. The fountains of your heart were broken up. But you held out until the springs ran dry. Once you were interested in the Christian life and service. Now you are waiting for that old interest to come back to life. Thus, in one way or another, you excuse yourselves. Why! dear friends, does business refuse to go round in a circle; do meth.ds change; do things happen but once, and nothing repeat itself; are the drowsy and the careless left behind? And is there no progress in God's ways? Has His voice only one call? Is there no present requirement, no living, earnest, present necessity upon you if you would enter the kingdom of heaven? "Behold the bridegroom cometh!" What does that mean, except that you are to arise at once?

"Choose you this day whom ye will serve." What is that except you are to decide—to be wholly Christ's now?

This is God's method—to lay responsibility upon us, each for himself; to address us thus personally, as I am trying to address you, and to say: "Arise. Follow me. Shake off your lethargy. Make your decision, and do it now."

You have said a man must act upon PROBABILITIES. No business can be done otherwise. And there is no religion apart from faith. God says, "Trust me. There is my word; believe it, obey it, and thou shalt live." But you say, "I am not convinced. I want a certainty. I do not yet understand it all. I do not see through to the very end." No, you never will, and in your daily affairs you never do. Things are not so constituted.

Exactly in the line of what we have shown to be the underlying principle of daily life—namely, TRUST—God draws us to himself. We are to BELIEVE in Him, and because we believe in Him, we are to give ourselves to Him.

Have you done it? Come down to details. Look into your life, and into your heart. Are you living for God. really, truly? Not, are you professing to? But are you doing it? Are you looking after your motives, your purposes, your thoughts, your words? Are all made to tell for God and for Christ because you are His? If not, what? You could not succeed in business otherwise. Can you serve God, can you be truly His, without the same watchfulness of little things?

Be as liberal as you will in your judgments of others—are you exact with yourself? Ah, dear friends, how many deceive themselves here. You do not believe in eternal punishment for the impenitent sinner. You do not believe that God is angry with the wicked every day. Woe to you if you are taking advantage of your liberality to others to apply this doctrine to yourself. Where is the man who could hope to succeed in business on that principle? You never do it. You hold yourself to strictest accountability. You do not rest until you make every uncertainty tell in your favor. Suppose the word of God is true ; suppose that except a man believe on the Lord Jesus Christ, and go into the other world His servant, His child, he cannot be saved ; what then, dear friend? Where will you stand? You are dealing with a righteous as well as a loving God. An account is to be given to Him. Are you ready for it?

And are some of you ashamed to be Christians? You rejoice in your business. You are proud to be identified with it. You want to be known as one of the merchants, one of the manufacturers, one of the business men of St. Louis. You hesitate to be recognized as one of the Christians of St. Louis. Is there any thing nobler? "There goes A. B., one of our merchants, one of our lawyers, one of our bankers." Yes; but more than that, and before all that, "one of our Christians—a follower of the Lord Jesus Christ, a prominent believer, a conspicuous one." Why? Because his whole life proclaims it. He is a Christian with a purpose ; he believes in his religion, he stakes everything upon it, he glories in it, he lives up to it; and when he dies the town will lose in him, before all else, a man who loved the Lord Jesus Christ, and faithfully served him. Is not that something worth living for? Will you not, then, after this fashion, carry your business into your religion? Begin to be a Christian now, and be such a Christian that the angels and the little children may be glad over you.